THE WONDERS OF MANN

A guide to the curious places and mysterious features of the Isle of Man

Charles Guard

Culture
VANNIN

Published by Culture Vannin,
PO Box 1986, Douglas, Isle of Man IM99 1SR.

Front cover photograph: Glenn Whorrall
Title design: Ruth Sutherland

Printed and bound by
Words & Spaces, Douglas.

ISBN 978-0-9931578-5-1

Culture
VANNIN

THE WONDERS OF MANN

Introduction

The Isle of Man has been inhabited by mankind for nearly 10,000 years. During that time we have created some remarkable structures. The earliest remains are just simple flint tools for hunting and cooking, but during the Bronze and Iron Ages we created some impressive stone monuments, many of which survive today.

As civilisation developed, we started building defensive structures such as promontory forts and castles, and religious buildings such as keeills and churches. Housing, industrial buildings and quite a few eccentric items followed.

Nowadays, by a twist of fate, the Isle of Man is guardian to some extraordinary relics of the past such as the biggest water wheel in the world, a unique camera obscura, the oldest surviving electric tram system, the world's only horse tram system, the world's oldest continuous parliament, and much else besides.

This book is a celebration of all these wonders, natural and man-made.

Charles Guard.

THE WONDERS OF MANN

contents

calf of man lighthouses

a light for mariners on the dark seas

THE CALF OF MAN lighthouses were completed in 1818 and were designed by Robert Stevenson, the Chief Engineer of the Northern Lighthouse Board, based in Edinburgh. They were the first Manx lighthouses built by the Board and as well as marking the Calf, the two lights were aligned so that their beams pointed towards the treacherous submerged rock off the Calf called the Chicken Rock (*see page 8*).

They used the latest optics and were finished in stone imported from Scotland with many unique design features such as dolphins and the Three Legs of Man included in the ironwork. The copper roof of the light tower is a cleverly disguised chimney allowing the heat from the lamps to escape into the night air.

Inside the light room of the lower tower.

Calf of Man lighthouse

Chicken Rock lighthouse

the chicken rock lighthouse

one of the engineering marvels of the age

THE CHICKEN ROCK lighthouse was completed in 1874 to mark a dangerous reef off the south east of the Calf of Man. It was engineered by the famous Stevenson brothers whose family had built most of the lighthouses throughout Scotland and the Isle of Man.

It is 144 feet tall and the first thirty-two feet of the tower are solid stone. Its foundations go 12 feet into the rock and contain over 1,000 blocks of interlocking granite. Such construction is needed to withstand the fierce battering from the many winter storms.

The light is now automatic but at one time three keepers lived in the tower, doing shifts of eight weeks on and four weeks off. In December 1960 there was a fire in the tower and the keepers were forced to retreat into the light chamber at the top. They were eventually rescued by the nearby lifeboats and none suffered any serious injury.

Chicken Rock during construction.

the point of ayre

a part of the island on the move

THE POINT OF AYRE is the Island's most northerly point and it seems it's on the move. An aerial photograph of 2016 has been overlaid with the earliest Ordnance Survey of 1868 and it shows a dramatic movement of the shingle beach round to the south east in the past 150 years.

As the tide pulls sand and stones up the west coast the heavier material is deposited at the Point, and the sand is dragged out into the Irish Sea, forming underwater banks that can be a hazard to shipping.

It is intriguing to imagine what the Point might have looked like 400 years ago when John Speed produced his map of the Isle of Man (*right*). His surveying might have been more accurate than we give him credit for - the intervening centuries might have moved the Point to where it is today.

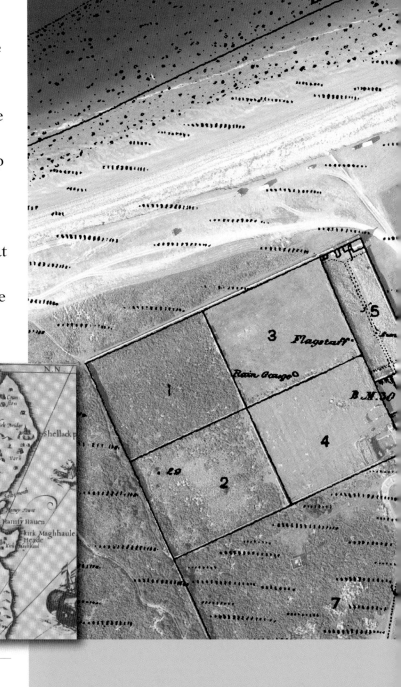

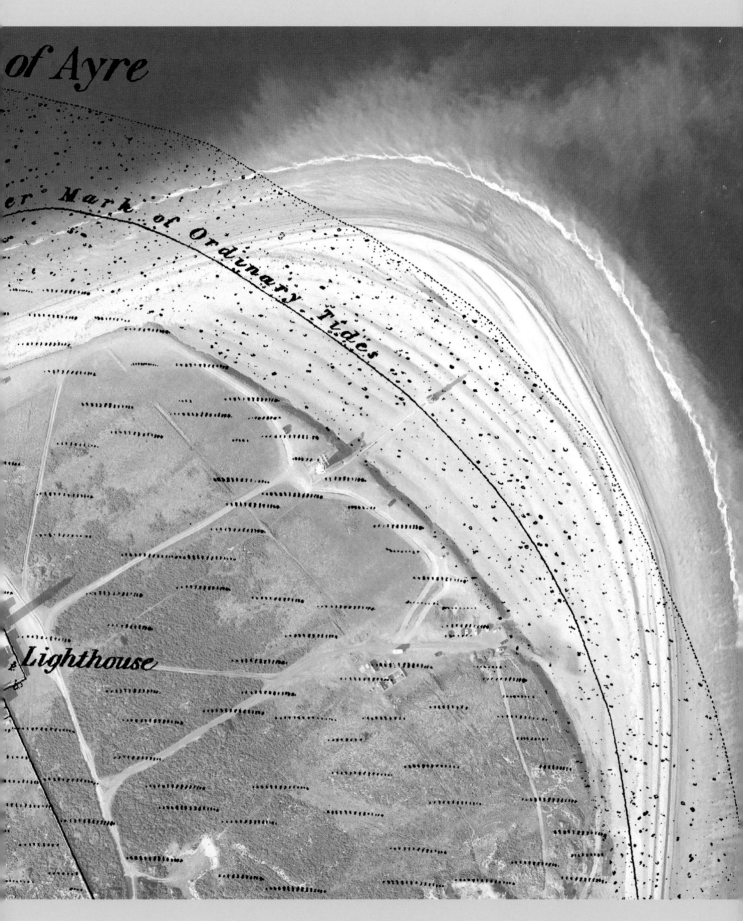

er Mark of Ordinary Tides

Lighthouse

Lighthouses
Old and New

TWO LIGHTHOUSES were completed on the Calf in 1818, not just to alert mariners to the Calf itself but also, cleverly, to mark the treacherous Chicken Rock just off its coast (*see page 6*).

The two Calf lights were synchronised so that they always shone in the same direction as they turned. When the mariner saw that one light was directly above the other then he knew that the Chicken Rock was in line between him and the Calf and, assuming he was well out to sea, he could sail past safely.

Each light had its own keeper's house which was beautifully fitted out with fine quality panelling and all the facilities that a family would need.

Sadly, the interiors were badly vandalised in the early 1990s and little now remains of the superb woodwork that had survived since 1818.

The interior of the lower house, sadly vandalised.

THE CURVED STAIRCASES that led to the light rooms were once panelled in wood by the finest craftsmen, brought over from Scotland. Little now remains of this work and in the lower light (*left*) the panelling was stripped off and sold for firewood in the 1990s.

The Winkie and the single foghorn in the early 1900s.

AS THE POINT OF AYRE has moved over the centuries (*see page 10*) the original lighthouse, built in 1818, found itself further inland and so, in 1899, an auxilary light had to be built 750ft to the east. Nicknamed 'The Winkie' it originally stood next to a single foghorn, but as the shingle bank continued to grow The Winkie was moved a further 250ft towards the sea and increased in height. Nowadays The Winkie is no longer needed and is in private ownership.

Tower of Refuge, Douglas

the tower of refuge

one man's vision
to save sailors

BUILT IN 1832 on exposed rocks at the entrance to Douglas harbour, the Tower of Refuge was the response of Sir William Hillary to the appalling loss of life from shipwrecks he witnessed from his house on Douglas Head. Sir William had frequently led men in rowing boats on heroic rescue missions, and his work inspired him to found the Royal National Lifeboat Institution. After leading a particularly heroic rescue to the steamship *St George* blown onto the reef during a fierce gale during which he was seriously injured, Sir William raised the funds to commission local architect John Welch to design a gothic-style refuge for mariners stranded on the rocks during such storms. Although described by one visitor to the Island as 'rising from the water like a fairy palace from below' the tower nevertheless provided practical help for those in distress. A spiral staircase allowed survivors to climb up above the sea to where a bell was provided to draw attention to their plight, and there were even basic provisions on site so they could sustain themselves until a rescue could be attempted, and for nearly two hundred years the tower has defied the storms of Douglas bay, a tribute to both its architect and to its creator, Sir William Hillary.

Sir William Hillary.

Herring Tower, Langness

the herring tower

an **early** marker for **mariners**

KNOWN AS THE HERRING TOWER, this striking stone building stands on the flat promontory of land called Langness. No one ever looked for shoals of herrings from it - not a very practical idea. Rather, its purpose was to mark the stretch of low land before the days of lighthouses. The herring fleet returning to the safety of Derbyhaven Bay would have used it to guide them on gloomy days when the features of the land weren't clear, though during the herring season the entrance to the bay was also marked by a temporary light attached to the Derby Fort.

The Herring Tower was designed by Thomas Brine, an English architect who established himself in Castletown. Its date is uncertain but it was probably constructed around 1811. It has a treacherous spiral staircase inside which is best avoided.

Marker
Towers

Long before lighthouses were common, mariners would use any man-made landmark they could to help them navigate. Towers were particularly useful

CORRIN'S FOLLY was built by Thomas Corrin in 1806. He lived in nearby Knockaloe and, as he owned the hill, built the tower on his favourite spot. Thomas was a Congregationalist and apparently wanted nothing to do with the established church and so was buried in the ground next to the tower along with his wife and two children. During his life Mr. Corrin used to spend a lot of time reading in the room on the third floor of the tower where there is a fireplace in one of the corners. However, the light from the tower could be seen for quite a distance out to sea and returning fishermen sometimes confused it with the Peel breakwater light. As a result of complaints the Government made him seal up the windows, which is how it remains today.

MILNER'S TOWER stands on top of Bradda Head, 382ft above the sea. It was built in 1871 as a gesture of gratitude from the people of Port Erin to William Milner, a maker of fire-resistant safes in London, Manchester and Liverpool. He moved to the Island and became known as the godfather of Port Erin due to his charitable work, especially in supporting poverty-stricken fishermen. The tower is built in the shape of an old-fashioned key.

Finally, there's the small tower in the Villa Marina gardens. No one seems to know who built it, when or why.

AS WELL AS building the Herring Tower on Langness (*see page 16*) Thomas Brine built a similar tower on Douglas Head at about the same time. It was also a marker, to help mariners distinguish similar headlands nearby as they made their way to Douglas. The tower still stands but has been incorporated into the Douglas Head apartments. This archive photograph shows the tower when it was part of the Douglas Head Hotel. It's a WWII photograph showing the naval radar training school, HMS *Valkyrie*.

milntown mill

wheels and cogs that supply power

RECORDS SHOW THAT there have been mills associated with the Milntown estate since the early 15th century. Parts of the present building are said to date back to that time and milling was certainly taking place on the estate up to 1930 when, after a catastrophic flood that damaged many properties in Glen Auldyn, the mill was put out of action.

The estate's last private owner, Sir Clive Edwards, undertook extensive repairs of the building and its machinery and in 1966 the restored mill was reopened. At the ceremony was Joe Keig, the last miller to work there before the 1930 flood.

As Sir Clive didn't want to mill flour, he connected the wheels and gearings to machinery more useful to his interest in cars and bikes. The water wheel now powered an electric generator, a compressor and overhead belts connected to drills and lathes.

Milntown mill

energy from waste plant

an efficient solution for the island's waste

THE ENERGY FROM WASTE FACILITY (or the incinerator, as it is popularly known) at Richmond Hill was completed in 2004 and deals with nearly 50,000 tons of domestic and clinical waste each year. As the lorries arrive on site they tip their contents into a huge concrete-lined bunker which can hold up to 16 days' waste. A giant grab crane mixes the waste and every few minutes lifts a load up and drops it into a hopper that feeds the furnace, where it is burned at temperatures of over 850°C. Clinical and animal waste is burned in a separate furnace which reaches temperatures of over 1,000°C.

The heat from the furnaces is used to drive a steam turbine which generates electricity which is fed into the Island's national grid. 10% of the Island's electricity is generated here. The design of the plant allows rainwater to be collected and used for cooling processes and for driving the turbine. The inert bottom ash is sent to a landfill site at Ballasalla and the toxic residues from the filters in the chimney are sent to a licensed facility in the UK for safe disposal.

Energy From Waste Plant

Lime Kilns, Scarlett

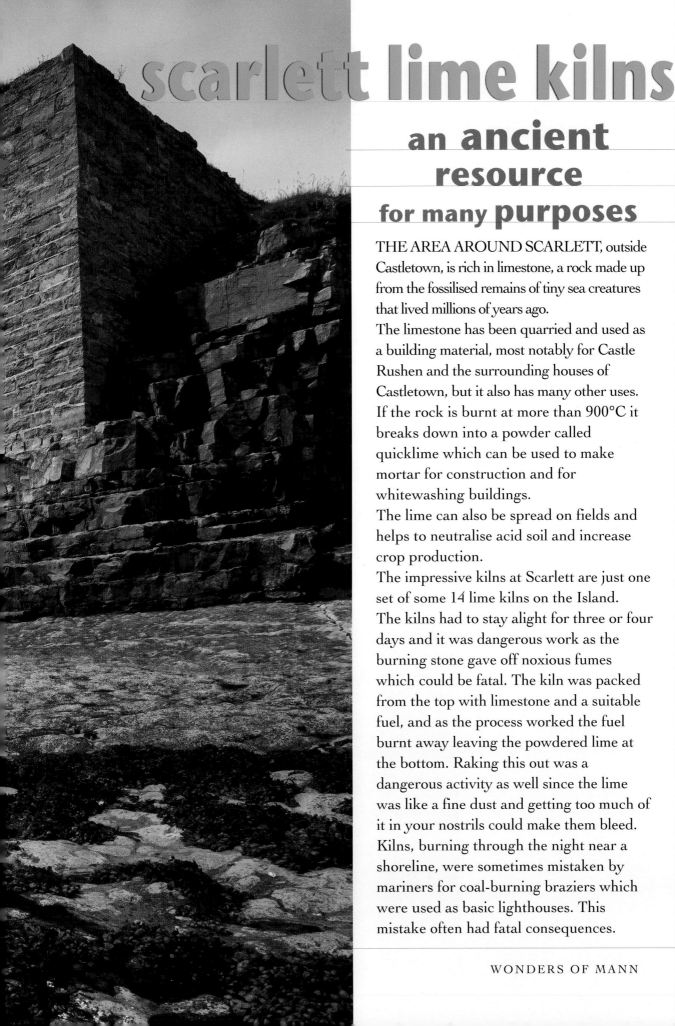

scarlett lime kilns
an ancient resource
for many purposes

THE AREA AROUND SCARLETT, outside Castletown, is rich in limestone, a rock made up from the fossilised remains of tiny sea creatures that lived millions of years ago.

The limestone has been quarried and used as a building material, most notably for Castle Rushen and the surrounding houses of Castletown, but it also has many other uses. If the rock is burnt at more than 900°C it breaks down into a powder called quicklime which can be used to make mortar for construction and for whitewashing buildings.

The lime can also be spread on fields and helps to neutralise acid soil and increase crop production.

The impressive kilns at Scarlett are just one set of some 14 lime kilns on the Island. The kilns had to stay alight for three or four days and it was dangerous work as the burning stone gave off noxious fumes which could be fatal. The kiln was packed from the top with limestone and a suitable fuel, and as the process worked the fuel burnt away leaving the powdered lime at the bottom. Raking this out was a dangerous activity as well since the lime was like a fine dust and getting too much of it in your nostrils could make them bleed. Kilns, burning through the night near a shoreline, were sometimes mistaken by mariners for coal-burning braziers which were used as basic lighthouses. This mistake often had fatal consequences.

old chemical works
a remote place to burn seaweed

THIS STRANGE WALL sits on the beach below the north side of Maughold Head. It's most easily reached by kayak, though you can clamber down from the coastal footpath high above. Marked on the 25in Ordnance Survey map as 'The Chemical Works' the massive structure was apparently built to extract iodine from seaweed. The weed was cut from the nearby rocks at low tide and then burnt in a circular pit. It smouldered for a day or so leaving lumps of ash that could be simmered in hot water and then filtered; a concentrate of iodine was the result. 24 tons of seaweed produced just 8 lbs of iodine. However, the positioning of this plant, on an almost inaccessible beach, is a real mystery. Surely it would have been much easier to treat the seaweed on Ramsey beach? And why was the massive wall, which seems to be holding back the land behind, necessary? Most of it has now collapsed, but in places it rises up nearly 20ft. At the southern end there is a carefully built archway which leads in behind the wall to the remains of what looks like a tall chimney. In 1871 the census names a certain Edward Vonstadt, as 'Chemical Manager, employing 2 men'. He lived with his wife Mary in nearby Elgin Cottage.

Chemical Works, Maughold Head

the bellite factory

a scheme foiled by tynwald

This strange concrete structure, hidden in the woods above Cornaa beach, dates from the 1880s and has a bizarre history. Over in Sweden a new explosive had been invented by a Mr Carl Lamm which he called Bellite. It had unique qualities: it could be hit with a hammer or set on fire and it wouldn't react, only a specialised detonator could make it explode; it was therefore much safer to handle and use than dynamite. Mr Lamm wanted to move to England to manufacture Bellite but English law prevented him, so he decided to build a factory in the Isle of Man where there was no legislation governing the manufacture of explosives. He started to build his plant at Cornaa but was stopped by the Governor, Spencer Walpole, who said he would need to examine the process first. A Select Committee was set up to hear witnesses but the members of the Keys also wanted their own Select Committee so they took evidence as well. Soon it ended up as a battle of wills between the Keys and the Governor and almost caused a constitutional crisis. The whole process took nearly five years, by which time Mr Lamm had long since abandoned his plans, withdrawn his workmen and his money and left the Island. The factory was never finished, nothing was ever made there and the Island still has no legislation governing the manufacture of explosives.

Carl Lamm.

Bellite factory, Cornaa

south bradda mines
mining
since the
the bronze age

CLINGING TO THE ROCKS at the bottom of Bradda Head is a chimney and the remains of stone buildings. It was to here that miners made their way, down a precarious footpath, to enter the adits and shafts of the South Bradda mine. Rising up behind the chimney is a huge quartz vein, once described by Sir Warrington Smyth, the Victorian president of the Geological Society as 'the noblest surface exhibition of a mineral vein to be seen in Europe'. Indeed, from earliest times this has been an attractive place to miners. An ancient maul, or tool for breaking off rock, possibly dating from the Bronze Age was found on the beach, indicating that this place has been mined for its minerals for over three thousand years. The rocks have yielded copper which, when mixed with tin or zinc produce the metal known as bronze.

The chimney is next to a building which once housed a steam winding engine, probably used for pulling up the ore from deep underground. The scenery here is certainly dramatic. The path to the mine passes a small stone building where the mine captain would have had his office and this sits on top of a huge natural arch.

South Bradda Mine

north bradda mines

an engine house
clinging to the
rock face

ROUND THE HEADLAND from the South Bradda mine is an even more remote and unlikely place for miners to access. Sitting at the bottom of cliffs that tower nearly 300 feet above is the remains of an engine house which was built in the 1860s to pump water from the shafts below. It could pump 200 gallons of seawater a minute from a depth of over 400 feet from the shafts that ran out under the seabed. Access to the mine is down a zig-zag path which starts through a cleft in the cliffs above. The path passes what appear to be small caves and they are thought to be trial adits made by the monks of Rushen Abbey in the 13th century. Nowadays much of the path has been washed away and the descent is extremely treacherous, and even when you reach the shore, scrambling along to the engine house is hard work. It's difficult to imagine how the steam engine was delivered to such a remote place, and how the ore was transported away for treatment, especially on the many days when access by sea would be impossible due to the weather.

The mine was run sporadically over many years and never seems to have made huge profits. The cliffs at sea level are covered with vivid green stains from the copper ore, and it's this that must have attracted the early miners.

North Bradda Mines

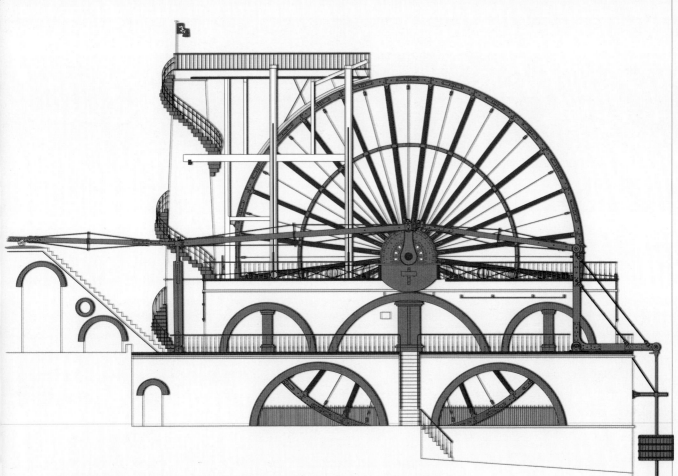

THE GREAT LAXEY WHEEL is, quite simply, the greatest waterwheel in the world. Built in 1854 to pump water from the lead and silver mines at Laxey, it was designed and engineered by Manxman Robert Casement, born in Lonan. Its personal details are impressive. It has a diameter of 72ft 6in and round its rim there are 168 compartments, or buckets, which collect the water which is gravity fed up the tower at the back and which runs along the viewing platform and falls onto the wheel. It is the weight of this water in the buckets that makes the wheel turn. The massive axle is 17ft long and weighs 10 tons. Running from a crank attached to the axle is a rod, supported by stone arches, which is more than 670ft long. The rod is attached to the top of the pumping mechanism which goes down some 1500ft underground and it is from these depths, where the miners worked, that the great wheel brought up the flood waters, day and night.

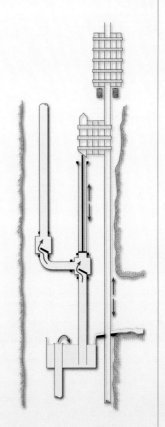

Diagram of one of the pumps

Robert Casement.

THIS EXTRAORDINARY PIECE of machinery (*left*) is in a chamber 150ft below ground in the Laxey mines. It is in fact a giant counterweight for the man engine (*right*) which was a water-powered machine that lifted and lowered a rod, 1200ft long, that took the miners down to the lower shafts. Miners stepped on and off small platforms attached to the rod as it was lifted and lowered in 12ft strokes. It took 25 minutes to reach the bottom, but this was an improvement on the 60 minutes it took using ladders. All this machinery was lowered down the shafts and assembled by the light of candles, an extraordinary feat in itself, but this counterweight is only one of three: the others are even deeper underground, the lowest being a thousand feet down.

The Manx Diocesan Crozier

A fine example of silver from the Laxey mines can be seen in the Bishop's crozier, or pastoral staff. Made in 1908 and designed by architect William Caroe, the silver is beautifully worked and combined with a piece of Manx bog oak, dug up from the curraghs near Ballaugh. One side of the ornate head features the arms of the diocese of Sodor and Man, and other side (*right*) features an image of St Maughold, adrift in his coracle on the way to the Isle of Man. The Bishop's mitre above the shield features the Three Legs of Man as well as swastikas, an ancient sacred symbol in use long before it was misappropriated by the Nazis.

manx electric railway

a transport wonder from the victorian age

THE MANX ELECTRIC RAILWAY is the longest narrow gauge vintage electric railway system in the British Isles, and the oldest such in the world. It still uses its original Victorian and Edwardian rolling stock and two of the trams in use are the oldest regularly operated tram cars in the world. Trams 1 & 2 were the first cars used on the line and started their service in 1893 when the newly opened line reached as far as Groudle. Next year the line reached Laxey and by 1899 it was in Ramsey. These early cars were built by Milnes of Birkenhead and have superb, wood-panelled interiors with each window having a mirror panel above it. The new tramway soon became the most popular tourist attraction on the Island. It carried hundreds of thousands of passengers each year, and some days so many people were waiting to board the trams at Derby Castle that visitors booked a ticket and took a horse tram back along the promenade to the end of the queue.

Electric Car interior

Manx Electric Railway

THE EXTRAORDINARY electrical system that powers the Manx Electric Railway includes giant bulbs with bubbling mercury inside. They were used until recently to convert the railway's electricity supply from AC to DC. Although they are now decommissioned it's hoped they will be retained and used as part of a museum display in Laxey. These mercury arc rectifiers are now extremely rare.

ONE OF THE MORE unusual transport items to be seen on the Isle of Man is the world's smallest production car, the P50, made in Peel. Founded in the 1950s by Cyril Cannell, Peel Engineering produced over 50 of these tiny glass fibre cars which did over 100 miles to the gallon and had a top speed of 40mph.

THE ISLAND IS RICH in unusual transport and 2016 saw the 140th anniversary of the Douglas Bay Tramway. There are very few other horse-drawn tramways in the world and the one in Douglas is the last remaining 19th century original. Built in 1876 by Thomas Lightfoot, an engineer who had retired to Douglas with his wife and thirteen children, it remains one of the iconic features of the Isle of Man. By the late 1890s the tramway was carrying in excess of one-and-a-half million passengers and even today it remains a popular tourist attraction. Long may it continue.

peel pipe organ
painted pipes
and
sweet sounds

THE PIPE ORGAN in Peel Methodist Church is just one of more than sixty pipe organs on the Isle of Man, most of them in churches and chapels, but some in private homes as well. They often have wonderfully painted pipes, impressive wooden cases and a commanding sound. Although most of the instruments were designed and built by English organ builders, some of them were actually built by a local builder, a Mr Moses Morgan of Athol Street in Douglas. Before electricity became commonplace in Manx churches the organs were often pumped by hand – a member of the congregation or a choirboy taking a turn at the back-breaking task during the hymns. However, some churches installed more sophisticated machinery such as that in Castletown Methodist Church where a water engine, (*right*) powered by the local water supply, was used to drive a pump which filled the air reservoirs ready for the organ to sound.

Peel Methodist Church

ech,
al art
uen.

Lo, a great Multitude, which no man could number, of all Nations, and Kindreds, and Pe
with white robes, and Palms in their hands; and cried with a loud voice, saying,
the Lamb. These are they which came out of great tribulation, and have washe

26, 27, 28.

st thomas' church

a great multitude which no man could number

THE CHURCH OF ST THOMAS, at the bottom of Crellin's Hill in Douglas, was opened in 1849 and provided a place of worship for the north end of Douglas, which was rapidly expanding in response to tourism. The walls inside were originally painted plain white but Canon Savage, the vicar there in the 1890s, decided that a grand scheme of elaborate murals should be undertaken and he commissioned the Island's foremost artist, John Miller Nicholson, to do the work.

The result is a masterpiece, combining religious symbols and events from the Bible along with stunning artwork and majestic design.

The wall opposite the organ depicts a scene from the Book of Revelation where a great multitude of 'all nations, and kindreds, and people, and tongues, stood before the throne, and before the Lamb, clothed with white robes, and palms in their hands'.

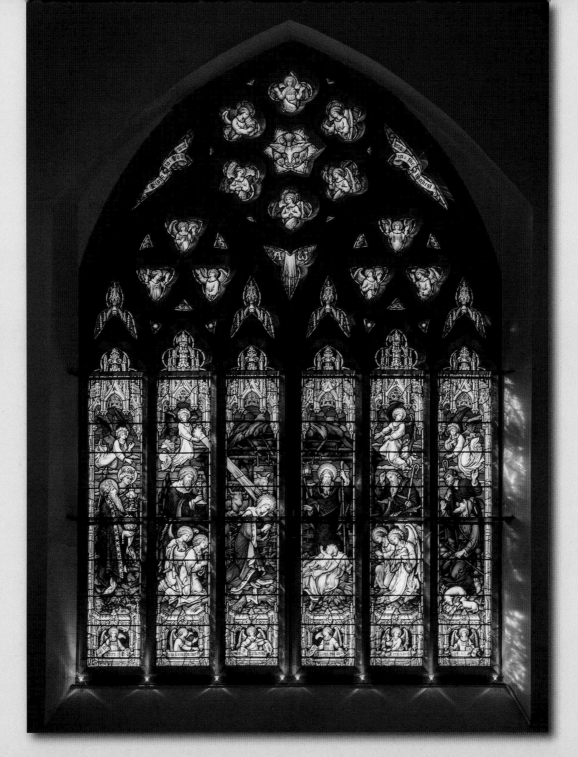

THE ISLAND'S MANY CHURCHES contain some superb stained glass. They depict a wide variety of topics including biblical scenes, the lives of the saints the churches are dedicated to, and memorials to parishioners. Others depict scenes from the life of the parish.

There are windows by some major artists and designers such as Giles Gilbert Scott, architect of the anglican cathedral in Liverpool.

The photograph on the left is made up from panels to be found at the east end of Maughold Church. The outer panels feature lilies and the centre panel shows pomegranates.

The photograph above is of the west end of Peel Cathedral. The window, which depicts The Nativity, replaced an earlier window which was blown out during a catastrophic storm in 1903.

Paintings
and pipes

Splendid organ cases and intricate machinery are a feature of many of the Island's churches

ON THE OPPOSITE page is the superb pipe organ in Trinity Methodist Church in Douglas. Built in 1899, the instrument is one of the finest on the Island and its case, made from pitch pine with beautifully decorated pipes, dominates the west end of the church.

The largest of the Island's pipe organs is that in St Thomas' Church in Douglas (*left*). Surrounded by the murals of John Miller Nicholson (*see page 43*) depicting angels blowing trumpets, the instrument has three keyboards and over two thousand pipes. Its interior is quite extraordinary: the pipes from one of the trumpet stops (*bottom left*) present a bizarre sight with their curved tops, and the reservoirs of air (*below*), ready to supply the pipes when they sound, sit beneath rows of beautifully organised mechanism.

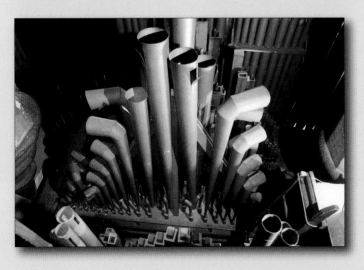

south barrule hill fort

South Barrule

a village
on a hilltop
in ancient times

SOUTH BARRULE dominates the south of the Isle of Man. Its heather covered sides lead to an extraordinary Bronze Age fortified village on its summit. Nowadays, only small indentations in the ground are visible, but

at one time over 70 round houses stood here, defying the Manx wind and rain. The houses had stone floors and were probably built of daub and wattle with thatched roofs. The entire village was surrounded by a huge stone rampart, much of which is still there, although it has long since tumbled into the grass.

However, if you walk along its remains it is possible to get an idea of the amount of stone that was used in its construction and if all the fallen stones were built up again the height of the rampart might be as great as twelve feet. More than this, it seems that there was once an inner rampart as well which might have been defended by large wooden poles, sharpened at their ends and pointing towards any attackers. It is probable, though, that the stones from this rampart were moved and reused in the later, larger defence which might indicate that as more people came to live on the summit the site had to be increased.

PLACED in such an inaccessible and remote location, its construction must have been a major operation for the small population that was on the Island at the time. Given the inhospitable conditions on the summit of South Barrule it is also possible that it was only inhabited in times of extreme threat from other tribes on the Island. Bringing food to the summit would have been a major exercise as would the quarrying and shaping of the thousands of stones needed to build the rampart.

A forgotten place of refuge.
(*Above*) An artist's impression of what the great rampart around the summit might have looked like; (*below*) over seventy hut circles have been identified and when inhabited there would have been a considerable village within the walls; (*opposite*) an aerial view of the summit of South Barrule. The remains of the rampart are clearly visible and some of the ancient hut circles can also be seen.

Castle Rushen

the best preserved medieval castle in europe

THE OLDEST PART of this remarkable castle is thought to date from the late 1100s but since then there have been many rebuilds and additions as towers were added, walls raised and outer defences strengthened.

The castle was attacked by French pirates in the 14th century and laid siege to by Robert the Bruce, but through all this it has been a seat of power for the rulers of Mann, most notably the Stanley family, better known as the Earls of Derby.

As supporters of the Royalist cause in the Civil War they held court here and offered shelter to other Royalist families who fled England. When the Lordship of Mann was abolished in the 18th century, the castle became the Island's main prison and sessions of the Manx Parliament, Tynwald, were held here as well as regular sittings of the courts. Nowadays it is a major tourist attraction.

Castle Rushen as a prison in Victorian times.

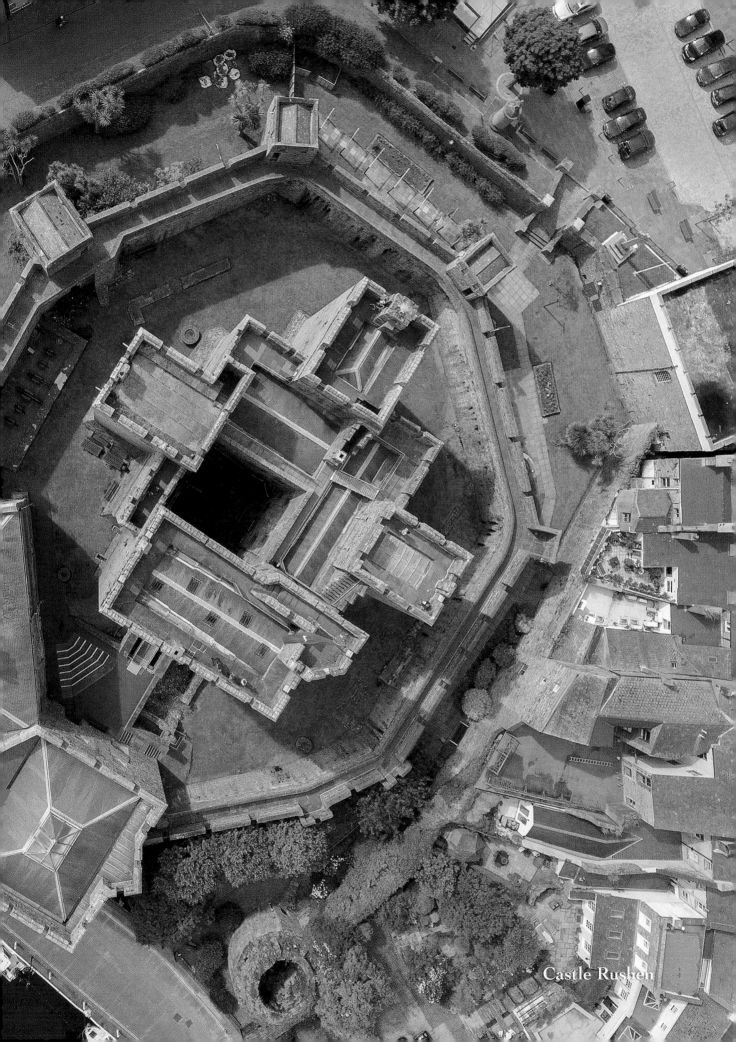

Castle Rushen

Kerroogarroo Fort

civil war fort

a defence against cromwell's army

BUILT BY THE 7TH EARL OF DERBY in the 1640s, Kerroogarroo Fort was part of His Grace's defences for the Island in case of attack by Cromwell's forces. It is a massive earth construction, with diamond-shaped bastions at its corners. These would have given the occupiers the advantage of being able to fire down on any attackers who might be trying to climb up the banks between. It's thought the fort would have had a strong wooden paling fence running round its top, and there would probably have been some wooden buildings inside for those garrisoned here.

During the Manx Rebellion of 1651, William Christian (Illiam Dhone) and his supporters took over most of the Island's forts from forces loyal to the Earl of Derby. The rebels were preparing to surrender the Island to the Parliamentary forces which were expected to arrive as a result of the Earl having been captured and executed in England a few weeks earlier.

Although there was some shouting and threats at the gate, the fort surrendered to Christian's men with no blood shed. Five days later the Parliamentary forces arrived in Ramsey bay and took control of the Island.

Historic
Sites

The Isle of Man has many historic sites, and the castles and forts dotted across the countryside are perhaps the most fascinating

ST PATRICK'S ISLE at Peel has a history going back thousands of years. The earliest remains indicate it was occupied as far back as the Mesolithic Age, between 8,000 and 4,000 years ago. The most visible remains date from the 10th century and include the round tower and St Patrick's Chapel. The ancient cathedral dates from the 13th century as do the earliest parts of the defensive walls which we now call Peel Castle. It was also used, from time to time, as a residence by the Lords of Mann.

THE CIRCULAR FORT on St Michael's Isle (*left*) was updated by the 7th Earl of Derby in the 1640s as a result of the fear of invasion from Cromwell's forces during the English Civil War; the Isle of Man was a Royalist stronghold and aggressive incursions were expected at any time. The fort's cannons all point across Derbyhaven Bay and no hostile ship could enter without being fired upon. The fort has many of the design features of a larger castle including a murder hole above the entrance door through which missiles could be dropped on anyone getting inside. There are also living quarters and an upper walkway with crenellations for firing down on attackers.

ONE OF THE most peculiar fortifications on the Island is Cronk Howe Mooar outside Port Erin (*left*). Nowadays it is a bracken-covered hill, but in fact it dates from the early 12th century and is entirely man-made. It is the site of an ancient motte and bailey castle. The motte, or hill, would have had some sort of fortified structure on it and the bailey, an enclosure running round the base of the hill, would have offered protection to people and livestock during a raid. An ancient Welsh chronicle records that in 1102 'Magnus, King of Germany, and with him a fleet, came a second time to Anglesey; and after felling for himself some trees for timber he returned to Man. And there he built himself three castles and a second time filled Man, which he had previously left desolate, with his men.' It could be that Cronk Howe Mooar was one of the castles that King Magnus built.

Artist's impression.

WWII bomb store

the island's contribution to WWII

DURING THE SECOND WORLD WAR the Isle of Man made an enormous contribution to the war effort. It was here that tens of thousands of military personnel were trained in all aspects of flying, radar operation and Morse code interception. New airfields were built at Andreas and Jurby where flight crews were trained in navigation, gunnery and bombing. At the side of Jurby Airfield is the bomb store, specially built to house high explosives. The whole complex is surrounded by huge earthen walls with reinforced concrete pillboxes. Overhead are steel gantries across which bombs could be moved, using block and tackle, and loaded onto a waiting bomb trolley to be taken to the nearby aircraft.

Bomb store, Jurby

bride radar station

part of the the world's first radar

ON THE FLAT PLAIN north of the village of Bride is a series of concrete bunkers that date from WWII. Now overgrown with gorse they were once connected to giant masts in the nearby fields which sent and received radio pulses designed to detect oncoming enemy aircraft. Bride was part of a chain of such stations placed around the entire coast of Britain and there were another three on the Island at Dalby, Scarlett and Cregneash.

If enemy aircraft were on their way, and they could be detected up to 70 miles away, signals were sent immediately to a central location in the north of England. From here the information was sent on to airfields with fighter aircraft and, just as importantly, to cities such as Liverpool and Glasgow where air-raid sirens were sounded, giving time for civilians to take cover in air-raid shelters.

The bunkers were manned 24 hours-a-day by shifts of RAF personnel and the advanced warnings coming from these sites must have saved countless civilian lives.

Radar bunker, Bride

Historic
Radar

Part of the world's first functioning radar system was here, in the Isle of Man

ORIGINALLY, all the bunkers on the site near Bride were covered in huge camouflage nets tethered at the corners to make them difficult to see from passing German bombers. Lines of power and signal cables ran across the fields connecting the bunkers to the nearby masts, but after the war all of these were removed as were the masts and much of the equipment in the bunkers themselves.

Over 120 people worked at the station including radar operators, mechanics, clerks, butchers and cooks, stewards, telephonists, service police and gunners. Those working in the bunkers themselves were protected from any potential gas attack from German parachutists by an air filtration system some of which, more than seventy years on, is still there (*opposite page*).

THE LARGEST BUNKER on the site was where diesel generators were housed to provide emergency power. In the case of a breakdown in the Island's electricity supply these generators would kick in. The bunker, built with both brick and concrete, has a huge blast wall running round its circumference to limit the damage that would be caused by an accidental explosion of the fuel stored inside.

THERE WERE BOTH wooden and metal masts associated with the radar systems. This photograph (*right*) is of the masts at Dalby and a similar set would have dominated the skyline at Bride. They were all removed in the 1950s.

rue point raised beach

a striking legacy of the last ice age

DURING THE LAST ICE AGE, which lasted for more than 100,000 years, the weight of the ice was so great that it pushed down the earth's crust by up to 500ft.

It's estimated that the ice over the Isle of Man was up to a mile thick. As the ice melted and finally started to recede about 12,000 years ago, the land started to recover and rise as the weight was removed.

Standing at Rue Point today you can actually see evidence of this. To the right of the photograph is a line of low cliffs covered in dark green bracken which looks as though it has been eroded by the sea. In fact, the sea was there, but it was thousands of years ago. As the land has slowly lifted it has pushed the sea back and the area which is now between the sea and the cliffs is referred to by geologists as a 'raised beach'. The recovery is slow, as little as a few millimetres a year, so you won't notice it, but it will be going on for quite a while. Some geologists estimate that it will continue for another 10,000 years, so there's a lot more land to be lifted up yet.

Rue Point

north barrule

a quarry for the Manx crosses?

HIGH ON THE SLOPES of North Barrule is a strange geological feature: tens of thousands of huge pieces of slate, strewn along the south-facing side of the hill.

The phenomenon is barely visible from the road far below, but if you walk up there the stones present a formidable barrier on the way to the summit.

Geologists explain the stones as caused by what they call the 'freeze-thaw' action at the end of the last Ice Age, around 12,000 years ago. There was little vegetation at this time and the hillside was virtually an exposed cliff which had been gouged out by glaciers. As the hillside faces south it meant that during the daytime in the summer, snow and ice would melt. The water would soak into the bare rock and at night it would freeze and expand and break up the cliff into the large slabs that we see today. This might be the only place on the Island where rock can be found of the size matching the largest of the Manx stone crosses, such as those displayed in Kirk Michael church. They are of the same rock type and it therefore seems likely that the Vikings extracted stones here for their carvings.

Gaut's Cross, Kirk Michael.

North Barrule

the chasms
a landscape
on the
move

THE CHASMS is a popular place to walk and admire some extraordinary scenery, most notably, the great fissures in the rocks past which the footpaths carefully wend their way.

It's only when you see the whole area from above that you realize the fissures mark a giant section of cliff that is gradually detaching itself from the main land mass and preparing to crash down into the sea, hundreds of feet below.

It may be many thousands of years before there is any further movement, or there might be a slip of rock tomorrow - it's impossible to tell, but other, smaller sections directly above the sea are already teetering on the edge, and some have fallen to the beach in recent years.

Beds of quartzite with thin, slippery mudstone beds in between, sloping towards the sea, combine to make the whole area even more unstable.

Sea-worn rocks at the foot of the Chasms.

The Chasms

dark skies

a glimpse of the infinite at night

THE LACK OF LIGHT POLLUTION on the Isle of Man makes it a prime place for observing the night sky. It currently has 26 of the British Dark Skies discovery sites and it has some of the darkest skies in Europe.

On a clear night many astronomical wonders can be seen with the naked eye such as the Orion Nebula, the Milky Way Galaxy and the Great Andromeda Galaxy, whose light has been travelling to us for some 2.5 million years.

This photograph was taken on the Calf of Man with the silhouette of the ruined upper lighthouse pointing to the night sky.

It is perhaps appropriate to quote the opening lines of a poem by Robert Louis Stevenson, the grandson of Robert Stevenson who built this light in 1818. Taken from his collection *Songs of Travel*, it perfectly describes the awe of seeing an infinity of stars in the heavens:

> The infinite shining heavens
> Rose, and I saw in the night
> Uncountable angel stars
> Showering sorrow and light...

Calf of Man

ALTHOUGH THERE ARE long sandy beaches in the north of the Island, most of the Manx coast is known for its sea cliffs, coves and caves. South of Port St Mary there are some remarkable features including the huge weathered stack known as the Sugarloaf, home to countless guillemots and kittiwakes during the nesting season. On calm summer days the area is a favourite with divers and kayakers and right next to the Sugarloaf is a spectacular passage cave with three entrances. Here the rocks exposed at low tide are almost entirely covered with anemones and sponges, and as the sunlight hits one of the entrances the reflected light makes the interior glow pink, as though it were covered in coral. A nearby cave is altogether different. The sea swell going into the cave traps air inside making a great booming sound and it takes a certain amount of courage to kayak into the darkness to investigate.

ancient wall of lava

memory of a turbulent past

OF THE MANY TYPES of rock to be found on the Island perhaps lava from an ancient volcano is the least expected. At Scarlett, just south of Castletown, there is limestone, formed around 330 million years ago when the Isle of Man was near the equator and in tropical waters. Like the rest of the earth's crust, the Island has been constantly moving and reforming over millions of years and during that time there was a volcanic eruption here, the remains of which can be seen today. Sitting on top of the limestone is a huge wall of lava and just off the coast is a feature known as The Stack, in fact a plug of lava in one of the vents on the side of the volcano which, when it cooled, formed into columns of basalt. If you look closely you can see tiny holes in some of the rocks – vesicles, where bubbles of gas were released from the molten lava.

Scarlett

ballaglass glen

carpets of bluebells and mossy stumps

ONE OF THE GREAT GLORIES of the Island is its glens. Follow any river up from the sea and you are bound to come to one of these atmospheric places. There are 18 national glens in the Island and one of the most striking is Ballaglass Glen, midway between Laxey and Ramsey on the east coast. Its semi-natural woodland has a typical mix of trees for a Manx glen: mature beech and oak at its centre, with larch, pine, willow, ash and birch in other areas. Perhaps its most famous feature, though, is the dazzling carpet of bluebells which appear every May.

No one has written about the Manx glens more poetically than the Victorian novelist and playwright, Hall Caine. He describes them as the 'narrow, winding, sinuous, dark and slumberous glens. The thin thread of blue water leaping and laughing, gliding and babbling and brawling and whooping and stealing its various ways down from the mountain-tops to the sea-beach; the lines of trees on either hand that make the light of morning dim with over-shadowing leafage; the golden fuchsia here, the green tramman there…then the eye of the sun peering down in places into the slumberous gloom and the breeze singing somewhere above the tree tops to the voice of the river below'.

Ballaglass Glen

The Curraghs

secret curraghs walk

the mysterious world of an ancient land

IN THE AREA north of Sulby and Ballaugh is a truly mysterious place – the Curraghs. Hidden from the main roads and only accessible along narrow, winding tracks, this ancient landscape is strange indeed. Gorse, reeds and rushes crowd in around small, hidden fields. Wild flowers and birds are in abundance and exotic plants, such as New Zealand flax, and unusual animals like wild red-necked wallabies, can be seen here as well. The wallabies are descended from several that escaped from the nearby Wildlife Park years ago, and they are now thought to be the largest breeding colony in the British Isles. It's an Area of Special Scientific Interest because here, on occasion, can be seen the largest numbers of winter roosting hen harriers in western Europe, and a subspecies of the tiny Wren, thought to be unique to the Isle of Man.

One of the most striking features of the Curraghs is the abundance of the Royal Fern, one of the largest and most imposing of the European ferns, and in early spring they crowd in on the paths that wind their way through the willow trees amongst which it is easy to get lost.

wild orchids

an **abundance**
of
wild **flowers**

From late May to July the meadows deep in the Curraghs present a dazzling display of tens of thousands of orchids with a backdrop of cuckoo flower, yellow rattle, and later in the summer harebells, purple loosestrife and meadowsweet. These photographs show the heath spotted orchid, but there are another five species which thrive here and one of the nature reserves, Close Sartfield, attracts many visitors each year to see this remarkable sight.

The Curraghs is the Island's largest wetland. It's really a legacy of the last Ice Age when, after the melting glaciers had retreated, this whole area was water-logged. On some 17th century maps it's marked as a lake. Its peat bogs have been exploited for fuel and over recent centuries there have been various schemes to drain the area. Even so, much of the wetland still survives and it is one of the most extraordinary landscapes on the Island.

Close Sartfield

stormy seas
nature
in her
wilder moments

THE SEA WALL at Douglas occasionally takes a battering from winter storms, and sometimes waves rebounding from the wall clash spectacularly with waves on the way in.

The Loch Promenade, named after the Governor of the time, was built in 1878 to provide development space for much-needed boarding houses, in demand as tourist numbers grew. Before the promenade was built there was little protection from the sea, just a sloping beach which, in many cases, came right up to the backs of the houses along Sand Street – appropriately named and later renamed as Strand Street.

Some of the houses did share a basic sea wall and part of this is still visible in the lane that runs behind the Loch Promenade Methodist Church (*right*).

Douglas Bay

Unusual
animals

**We might not have badgers or moles on the Island,
but we make up for it with some rather unusual animals of our own**

THE BASKING SHARK is the world's second largest living fish and is seen off Manx waters throughout the summer months. It might look frightening but in fact it only feeds on plankton, drifting around with its mouth open and filtering out the tiny organisms with its array of gills. One specimen, caught off Canada in 1851, had grown to 40ft in length, weighing a staggering 19 tons, but more usually they reach a mere 26ft and weigh around 5 tons. They move down to depths of 3,000ft during the winter to feed on deep-water plankton.

THE STRIKING-LOOKING Loaghtan sheep is a special breed and is believed to have been on the Island for a thousand years or more. They usually have four horns, but on occasion both males and females can have six. The fleece of the Loaghtan is of a fine texture and rich brown in colour. The Loaghtans can shed their own fleece, essential in a wild flock with no shepherd to shear them.

BOTH GREY and common seals can be seen around the Isle of Man and one of the best places to see them is on Kitterland, easily viewed from the Sound. They are inquisitive and are often seen following kayakers or popping their head above water if they hear people talking on a beach.

PERHAPS the most iconic of all Manx animals is the Manx cat. Sociable and tame, often with a thick, double-layered coat, the reason they have no tails or only short stumps is put down to a genetic mutation, but it's quite clear there are other, more plausible reasons…

How Manx cats are made

MANX FISH.

milntown house

an **exuberant gothic masterpiece**

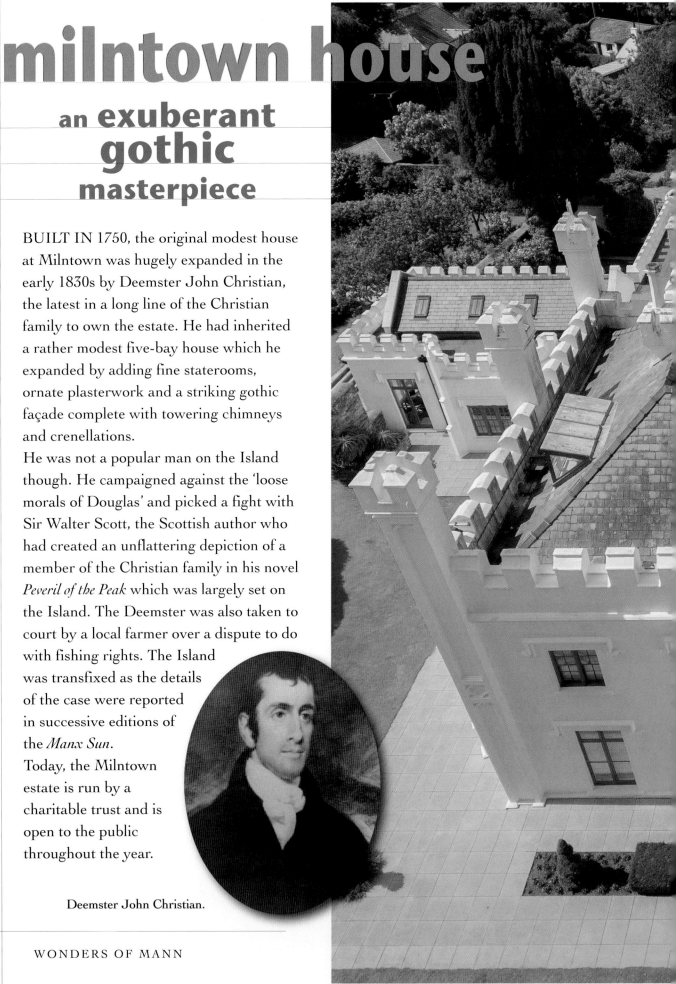

BUILT IN 1750, the original modest house at Milntown was hugely expanded in the early 1830s by Deemster John Christian, the latest in a long line of the Christian family to own the estate. He had inherited a rather modest five-bay house which he expanded by adding fine staterooms, ornate plasterwork and a striking gothic façade complete with towering chimneys and crenellations.

He was not a popular man on the Island though. He campaigned against the 'loose morals of Douglas' and picked a fight with Sir Walter Scott, the Scottish author who had created an unflattering depiction of a member of the Christian family in his novel *Peveril of the Peak* which was largely set on the Island. The Deemster was also taken to court by a local farmer over a dispute to do with fishing rights. The Island was transfixed as the details of the case were reported in successive editions of the *Manx Sun*.

Today, the Milntown estate is run by a charitable trust and is open to the public throughout the year.

Deemster John Christian.

Milntown House

loch hotel

florid architecture for a lost age

THE LOCH HOTEL on Loch Promenade in Douglas is part of a magnificent terrace of hotels built in the 1870s to accommodate the ever-increasing number of visitors to the Island. The visiting industry was to become the mainstay of the Island's economy for many years and it was a visionary Governor, Henry Brougham Loch, who pushed ahead the development of the town during the second half of the 19th century. The promenade was built on land reclaimed from the sea and the boarding houses give Douglas its distinct and splendid character. Although the terraces were designed by different architects, the fronts had to conform and be approved by an architect appointed to oversee the scheme. While there is variety amongst the designs, the overall unity has been described as 'the finest marine promenade in the world'.

Governor Loch.

Loch Promenade

Fantasies in cement

The tourist industry produced some of the most decorative and exciting architecture on the Island

ONE OF THE MOST ACTIVE developers in the late Victorian period was Alexander Gill. He was born in Onchan and educated at Onchan Parochial School. Although he trained as a bricklayer he soon saw the opportunities for developers as Douglas expanded through the Victorian and Edwardian periods. When he died in 1919 he owned 160 properties on the Island, many of them hotels or boarding houses. Typical of his seafront design is the Hydro Hotel, on Queen's Promenade. Above the top front window are his initials, AG, intertwined between the date, 1910. The front is full of decorative detail but it didn't stop there.

The main rooms, such as the lounge, smoke room and large dining room all have ornate plaster ceilings, a feature common to many of Gill's seafront hotels.

THE DOUGLAS BOARDING HOUSES were built for the booming tourist trade, to house people who came to the Island to enjoy themselves, to forget the drudgery of the factory and the daily grind and to have fun. The buildings reflect this purpose, and the terraces that grace the seafront at Douglas are masterpieces of decoration and elaborate design.

The Claremont is typical of the design detail that extends from pavement level right up to the top floor and beyond. The Douglas craftsmen who excelled in this work in cement could hardly be bettered anywhere.

EVEN IN VICTORIA STREET, leading on to the Promenade, ornate cement work was the order of the day. Perhaps the most flamboyant of them all is the façade of the Salisbury Hotel. Built in 1880 the detailing above the door depicts Helios, the personification of the Sun, driving his chariot. When the hotel was first opened it was called The Sun.

killabregga farmstead

a remote community on the uplands

HIGH ABOVE the winding road of Sulby Valley is an extraordinary series of abandoned farms, their roofs gone and their walls crumbling. There are 16 in all and they sit about 700ft above the valley floor. On a clear day you can see across the valley to the other farms, though access between them involves toiling up and down long, zig-zag paths that can still be seen on the hillsides. Life on these remote farmsteads must have been demanding and it is astonishing to realise that in the 1850s, according to a recently discovered diary, there were some 15 people living on the tiny holding of Killabregga. The two small dwelling houses had Mr and Mrs Kinrade and their four sons and four daughters in one, and in the other Mr Kinrade's mother and his three bachelor brothers and a spinster sister. Today it's just possible to pick out what the various ruined buildings were used for and there is still some rusting farm machinery lying around, such as the horse walk (*right*).

Killabregga, Sulby

ANOTHER ABANDONED farmstead at the height of 700ft, and just along from Killabregga is Craigmooar. It's hard to imagine the number of people who lived in the two dwellings here in the 1850s. In one house was John Quayle, his wife and five sons and two daughters and in the other was his mother, two daughters, one of their husbands and their sons.

At that time Craigmooar was not hidden amongst the trees of a plantation as it is today; crops were grown on the open hillside and they kept stock such as sheep, cattle, pigs and hens. Turf for fuel would be cut from higher up the hillsides.

The main dwelling house (*left*) has a strange addition to its interior; built around the fireplace at the far end is a thick wall forming a tiny room that would have been far too hot to sit in if the fire was lit. Its purpose is a mystery.

Its front and back doors are opposite each other. This arrangement was sometimes used to create a through-draught for winnowing grain when the weather was too wet to do it outside.

Craigmooar has a number of buildings as part of its complex and the presence of a cart house with a wide door indicates that the residents could afford more than just the pack-pony of some of the nearby farms.

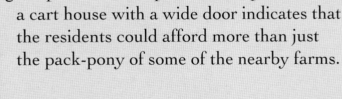

Unusual stone feature at Killabregga.

lonan wheel cross

a **unique** legacy of **carved** stones

THE ISLE OF MAN is particularly rich in carved stones from the Early Christian and Viking periods, and most of the ancient churches on the Island have displays of these remarkable artefacts.

One of the finest examples can be found at Lonan Old Church, dedicated to St Adamnan, a 7th century abbot of Iona. Dating from the early 10th century, this magnificent wheel-headed cross is believed to be standing in exactly the same position where it was placed some eleven hundred years ago.

It is decorated with a complex design featuring an equal-armed cross, filled with interlacing, set in a broad ring which is also decorated with more interlacing.

It is remarkably similar in design to a cross in Braddan Old Church, leading some to speculate that they may both have been created by the same person.

Lonan Churchyard

Historic
Sites

The Island has been occupied for nearly 10,000 years, and some of the early inhabitants left behind remarkable remains

HIGH ABOVE THE CORNAA VALLEY in Maughold is an ancient site known as Cashtal yn Ard, a Neolithic cairn dating to around 3000 BC. At one end there stands a series of tall stones, arranged in a curve. The two stones in the centre are low and close together and once formed a doorway. In its original form the cairn would have been entirely covered with earth, so entering through the doorway would have led you to a chamber inside which was divided into five smaller areas. These stone chambers originally contained burials and pottery.

LAG NY KEEILLEY, on the remote lower slopes of Cronk ny Arrey Laa, is one of the best preserved of the many keeill sites on the Island. You approach it along an old packhorse route which clings to the side of the hill. The keeill only comes into view at the last minute as you come to the brow of a steep incline, and from here you can see the whole site – the low walls of the keeill itself, two cairns and the remains of a priest's cell. Living on such a remote site must have been a challenge. There is a spring nearby and the possible remains of a small field for growing food, but given the westerly storms coming in from the Irish Sea during the winter months, any monk living here would have had his devotion sorely tested. There are some 170 known keeill sites on the Island, but only around 35 have any visible features. Archaeologists are undecided about their age. They are most likely from the early Medieval period and could range in date from the 8th to the 12th centuries.

IT IS OFTEN suggested by archaeologists that white quartz stone had some special significance for our remote ancestors. Certainly, if you drive up First Avenue off Glencrutchery Road in Douglas, you will see a very large example of this stone which has been carefully placed to great effect. It once stood on open land but now stands on a circular mound which juts out into the road. It was probably part of a larger ancient monument, and excavations in the 19th century revealed large quantities of prehistoric pottery in the area and close to the monument were found fragments of an urn and cremated human remains, typical of a Bronze Age burial.

tynwald day
a day of national celebration

THE NATIONAL PARLIAMENT of the Isle of Man, the Tynwald, was established by the Vikings over 1,000 years ago, and that makes it the oldest continuous parliament in the world. Each year, on 5th July, the Tynwald Ceremony takes place on the ancient tiered hill at the centre of the Island in St John's.

It's a day of pomp and ceremony and national celebration, with all the members of the House of Keys and the Legislative Council attending, along with the Lieutenant Governor, representatives from the Island's churches and various local authorities as well as distinguished guests from other countries.

The key purpose of the day is the promulgation of the Acts passed by the parliament during the previous year. The Island's two Deemsters read out the title and a short explanation of each Act, first in English and then in Manx Gaelic. The Acts are later signed by the Keys and the Council. Only then can they become law.

Tynwald, St John's

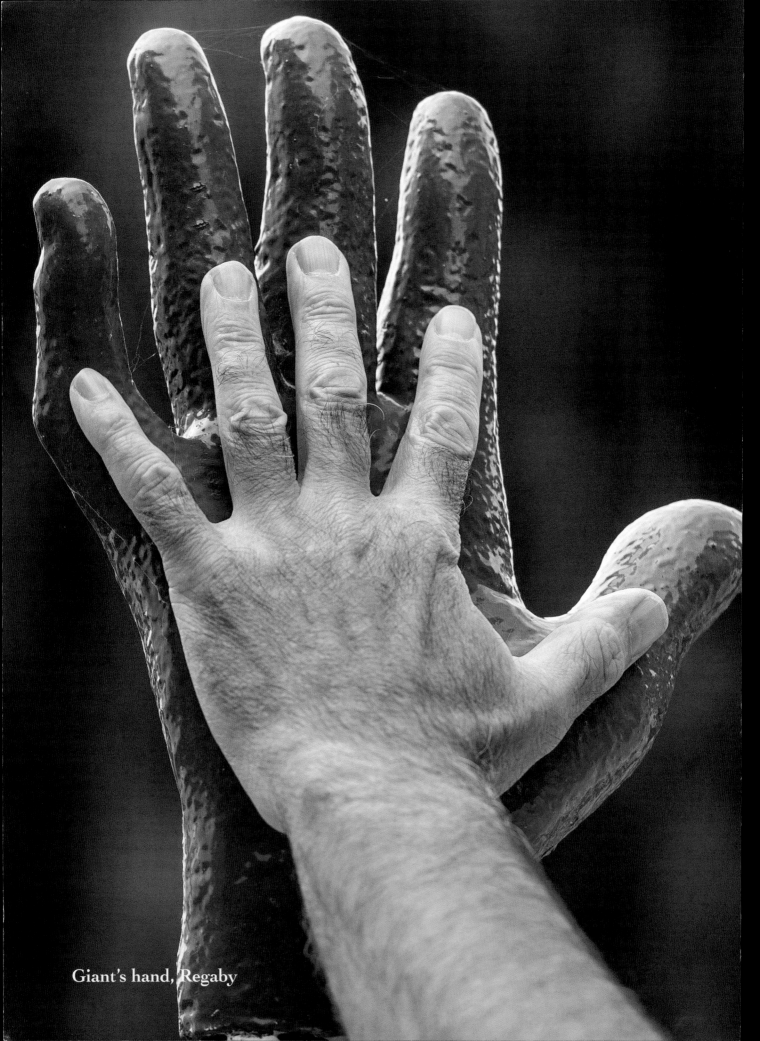

Giant's hand, Regaby

the giant's hand

the sulby man who became a legend

BORN IN A SMALL cottage in Sulby in 1824, Arthur Caley was one of thirteen children and he grew up to be the tallest man in the world reaching 7' 11" and weighing in at over 25 stone.

He left the Island at an early age to seek his fortune and before long was in Paris, being exhibited to great acclaim.

His death was reported there when he was only 28, but bizarrely he reappeared some time later in New York as a star attraction in Barnum's Greatest Show on Earth.

It's believed that his 'death' in Paris was part of an insurance scam.

He finally died in America in 1889 aged 64 and was buried in an unmarked grave in a small town in New Jersey. Before he left the Isle of Man in 1851 a cast of his right hand had been made and a number of copies produced. One of these adorns the gate pillar of Rose Cottage in Regaby. The tip of the middle finger is exactly 7"11" from the ground, indicating the height he reached when fully grown, though his military costume and plumed helmet would have added even greater height to this remarkable man.

gaiety theatre
victorian
stage machinery
unique in the world

THE GAIETY THEATRE in Douglas is one of the best preserved Victorian theatres in the British Isles. It has many wonders inside – its elaborate decoration, its remarkable ceiling and, not least, some unique stage machinery.

All of the traps, with their pulleys and counterweights, have been restored and are in working order and able to deliver good and bad fairies to the stage above during any pantomime; but there's one mechanism which is very rare indeed: the Corsican Trap. Originally designed for a special effect in a Victorian melodrama entitled The Corsican Brothers, this complex trap allows the actor to be gradually lifted up to the stage, moving across from one side to the other, through a gap in the floor which also moves. With the use of atmospheric lighting and a fog machine, a truly magical effect can be achieved.

Working model of the Corsican Trap showing how the actor is raised up from underneath the stage.

Gaiety Theatre, Douglas

Camera Obscura, Douglas

a camera obscura

a **way** to **spy** on the world **outside**

THE GREAT UNION CAMERA OBSCURA on Douglas Head is unique in the world, being the only one with eleven lenses. It's a Victorian marvel and was opened by a Rochdale entrepreneur, a Mr J R Fielding, in 1892. A series of mirrors, positioned in little dormers looking out across Douglas Bay, the harbour and the headland behind, reflect their images down through lenses to be projected onto white boards inside the building. The pictures are, of course, in full colour (*opposite left*) and moving, something which must have fascinated Victorian visitors to the site. Only when inside did they realise that everything outside was clearly visible to the hidden viewer, including the activities of courting couples.

a secret bank vault

an **eccentric** way of **keeping money** safe

HIDDEN AWAY in an extension on the side of Bridge House in Castletown is one of the most eccentric inventions on the Isle of Man.

It's a bank vault which can only be opened from the inside. Constructed by George Quayle for the Island's first bank in 1802, the mechanism was activated by dropping a ball into a tube in a room above and allowing it to make its way along various shutes until it dropped into the machinery in the vault. Its weight gradually turned a wheel that had a metal arm attached to it which, when lifted, allowed the door to be pushed open from the outside. It seems it was forgotten for many years and it was only opened again in the 1940s by taking out the lintel above the door and reaching inside to lift the bar by hand.

Bridge House, Castletown

bridge control building

a powerful machine
for douglas harbour

THE BRIDGE CONTROL BUILDING towers above the south side of Douglas harbour and inside is one of the most impressive pieces of Victorian engineering on the Island. Designed and built by the Armstrong Whitworth engineering company and installed in 1895, it provided instant power to swing the harbour bridge to the side to allow shipping access to the inner harbour. It worked on a clever principle. The huge red-painted accumulator was gradually raised up by a flatbed engine in the next chamber. The accumulator, which weighs some 40 tons, exerted enormous pressure on fluid trapped below. When the bridge needed to swing, the operator pulled a lever allowing the pressurised fluid to push mechanical rams that eventually pulled chains under the road causing the bridge to swing open.

The old swing bridge across Douglas harbour.

Bridge Control Building, Douglas

Historic
Machines

**Providing power for machinery and lighting was a
challenge in the times before any public supply of electricity in the Island**

THE ACCUMULATOR TOWER of the Bridge Control Building on Douglas harbour is a work of art in itself. Entirely functional, it is nevertheless beautifully designed and has become one of the icons of the harbourside.

The windows at the top gave the operator a perfect view of all movements in the harbour, and with the power stored in the accumulator below the swing bridge could be opened at a moment's notice.

The tower still has all its machinery in place but it is no longer used as the new lift bridge is powered in an entirely different way.

Its future is uncertain.

WHEN THE POWER from the accumulator was released it eventually activated these giant wheels which were driven by hydraulic rams. They, in turn, pulled chains under the road which turned the bridge.

The beauty of the system was that its power was available immediately; provided that the accumulator was raised and ready to go, the power it produced could be called upon at the pull of a lever, and there was usually ample time between passing vessels to lift it up again ready for its next turn.

LONG BEFORE there was a public supply of electricity on the Island businesses and wealthier residents had to generate their own. This flatbed engine was in an outbuilding on the Nunnery estate and was used to supply power to the main house as well as providing a belt drive to operate a circular saw in the next building.

The Photographers

We would like to thank the many photographers who have contributed to this book. They have often been intrepid, going to out-of-the-way places. They have flown in small planes, scrambled down cliffs, flown drones, kayaked to remote coastal locations and clambered down mines, all to capture the more remote wonders of the Island. The photographers and their images are listed below:

	Front Cover	Glenn Whorrall
1	Derby Fort	Glenn Whorrall
2	Maughold lighthouse	Duke Aerial Productions
4	Scarlett lime kilns	Simon Park Photography
6	Calf lighthouse	Glenn Whorrall
8	Chicken Rock lighthouse	Andrea Thrussell
10	Point of Ayre montage	Rob Clynes
12	Calf reconstruction	Andrew Martin
12/13	Lighthouse interiors	Glenn Whorrall
13	Lighthouses and foghorn	Author
14	Tower of Refuge	Simon Park Photography
16	Herring Tower	Glenn Whorrall
18	Corrin's Folly	Simon Park Photography
19	Milner's Tower	Simon Park Photography
19	Villa Marina tower	Author
20	Milntown mill machinery	Simon Park Photography
20	Milntown mill	Author
22	Energy from waste plant	Simon Park Photography
24	Scarlett lime kilns	Simon Park Photography
26	Old chemical works	Ian Comish
28	Bellite factory	Author
30	South Bradda mines	Author
30	South Bradda arch	Simon Park Photography
32	North Bradda mines	Glenn Whorrall
34	Laxey Wheel interior	Simon Park Photography
35	Laxey Wheel drawing & pumps diagram	Andrew Scarffe
36	Counterweight	Pete Geddes
37	Diocesan Crozier	John Hall
37	Man Engine	Pete Geddes
38	Car 1	Simon Park Photography
40	Cars 1 & 2	Simon Park Photography
41	Mercury arc rectifier	Alex Maddrell
41	P 50 & horse tram	Barry Edwards
42	Pipe organ and mechanism	John Hall
45	Murals	Andrew Barton
46/47	Stained glass	Patricia Tutt